Hidden Derby

Evening
Telegraph

Hidden Derby

The Breedon Books
Publishing Company
Derby

First published in Great Britain by
The Breedon Books Publishing Company Limited
Breedon House, 44 Friar Gate, Derby, DE1 1DA.
1999

ISBN 1 85983 181 8

Printed and bound by Butler & Tanner Ltd., Selwood Printing
Works, Caxton Road, Frome, Somerset.

Colour separations and jacket printing by
GreenShires Group Ltd, Leicester.

Foreword by Roy Christian

THE second thing to do on opening this book should be to cover over the captions temporarily and see how many of the subjects of the photographs you can identify.

The first thing you should have done, of course, was read this foreword; otherwise you may have deprived yourself of quite a lot of fun and perhaps a certain amount of chagrin for not getting more correct answers.

The next thing I must do is thank all concerned with the publication of this book for justifying my use here of that sentence so satisfying to the sender, yet so infuriating to the recipient: "I told you so."

What it is that I have been telling people – mainly adult students – to do when walking about Derby, is to look up above modern shop windows at what is often older and more interesting work. It may, in some respects, be unwise advice. It is liable to bring replies beginning: "I am writing this from a hospital bed because following your advice about looking up, I caught my toes on the raised edge of a paving stone and…"

I am sorry for the unfortunate consequence, but I continue to pursue my policy, which has also been the policy of the compilers of this fascinating book. They have looked not only upwards, but also downwards and sideways to find a Derby that is hidden from many of us because we have not bothered to look for it.

It is a policy directly opposite from that of the shop owners. They would have us fix our eyes on the shop window, especially on the goods so excitingly displayed in it. But I would have you concentrate on an upper window and its surrounds which may be centuries older and, to me, more rewarding.

A genuine example makes the point. If you pause at the east end of St James' Street to look across the Corn Market, you will have the entrance to Lock-Up Yard straight ahead of you. It probably dates from about 1830. The shop windows on either side were probably reinserted after the 1932 flood. The windows above them are unmistakably Georgian, as is the long narrow brickwork in which they are set.

This 18th-century upperwork is almost certainly a remnant of the townhouse of the Dukes of Devonshire. A residence for them in the county town would be essential in times when the present A6 trunk road was just a disconnected series of private ways and Chatsworth was almost a winter's day coach ride away. The introduction of steel springs to coaches late in the 18th century and improvements to roads early in the 19th made coaching quicker and more comfortable and reduced the need for town houses. Nearly all were eventually sold to business people who converted much of the ground floor to showrooms and used the rest of the building to house family, staff and stock.

But the home of the Franceys family a few yards further north where the Corn Market meets the Market Place, seems to have been built with business in mind in the 17th century. They were butchers and graziers then but bred a dynasty of apothecaries (chemists) who were the only family of trades people considered suitable to attend grand events in the early 18th century Assembly Rooms. Ownership changed but the business continued as a pharmacy until its window display, unchanged from 1865, was removed to Derby Museum. The four-storey building is still unchanged, though you have to cross the road and look up to appreciate its splendour.

But there can be few Derbeians who fail to look up at and appreciate the magnificence of the Cathedral's perpendicular tower. I suspect there may be many however who have never noticed the inscription carved in the stonework on a frieze at the top of the tower's lowest storey on the south side. "Young men and maidens," is what it says. What it means is anybody's guess. A tradition has it that the carver was trying to tell us that young people paid for that section of the tower, but nobody now believes this – except me and that is only because I can think of no better reason why a Tudor craftsman should waste valuable time and stone on part of a quotation from St Paul, quite meaningless as it stands, unless he was trying to tell us something. Shortage of cash may have been one reason why the second tallest parish church tower in Britain (as it was until it became a cathedral tower in 1927) took from 1509 to 1530 to build.

That is perhaps enough about looking up in Derby. You will need to look down below eye-level at times to make rewarding finds as well as to avoid occasional ill-fitting paving stones. And you may not, at first glance, always appreciate the importance of the object you are bending down to see. The single line of stones behind the rear windows of houses in Marcus Street, Little Chester, and the well on the lawn of St Paul's Vicarage close by, only become exciting when you know they are Roman and the sole visible remnants of Derventio outside the museum.

The Derby Civic Society's worthy but wordily titled Better City of Derby award paid for the recent restoration of a well in Well Street dedicated to St Alkmund, Saxon prince, saint and martyr. Ironically, St Alkmund's Church, which contained his mortal remains, had to be rebuilt on a new site to make way for an inner ring road in the 1960s.

Alongside the 18th and 19th-century turnpike roads, many cast iron mileposts survive, mostly made in local foundries. The one featured in Hidden Derby, showing Burton to be 11 miles away, is the most centrally situated of Derby's survivors.

But Derby has many interesting survivors, especially among its buildings. Unfortunately some of these may not continue to survive unless some appropriate use can be found for them.

Perhaps the finest of these is the Shire Hall (or County Hall) of 1659. It forms the centrepiece of a delightful group of three distinguished buildings in a courtyard on the north side of St Mary's Gate. Flanking it on the west is the former County Hotel or King's Arms of the 1790s; on the east is the Judges' Lodgings of 1811.

The Shire Hall was the legal, political, social and administrative centre of its county. Assize Courts were held there, Knights of the Shire (MPs) were elected there, the elite of the county and distinguished guests dined and danced there on special occasions.

The problem is now to adapt it to modern needs, while retaining some links with the law and avoiding major alterations to the splendid internal layout.

A totally different kind of building which presents a rather similar problem is the North Midland Railway Round House of 1839. One of the earliest round houses in the world, it may be the earliest survivor to retain its original layout. It cries out to be preserved, but for what purpose do you use a

Picture by Mike Inman.

A milepost on Green Lane provides the useful information to travellers that Burton is 11 miles away.

Picture by Mike Inman.

The grand entrance to Shire Hall, the old court buildings on St Mary's Gate, now overgrown with weeds.

giant turntable on which railway locomotives were originally reversed and was finally used in the 1980s for turning enormous cranes?

As a railway town, which to a reduced extent it still is, Derby has many impressive warehouses and other railway buildings. Some have been well converted to new uses, as a solicitors' office, for example, or a restaurant. Others seem to have been abandoned to damp and the vandals, like the one in Hidden Derby built in the 1870s alongside the Great Northern Railway line at the foot of Uttoxeter New Road.

Almost 40 years before that warehouse was built the North Midland Railway Company built, around what was to become the Midland Station, a colony for its workers. Recently, with a little pressure from the Civic Society, this delightful settlement has been refurbished, repopulated and elevated to conservation area status.

Indeed, after a century in which the city has lost too many good buildings, it has done much in the last 30 years to redress the balance. While it may be literally true to boast that Derby has more listed buildings than York, it would be economising with the truth to stress the point. York has fewer buildings altogether but more of top quality.

But Derby has more to offer than readily meets the eye. In Hidden Derby, you will find unusual events taking place in obscure places known only to the initiated; familiar spots viewed from unusual angles and dramatic views likely to be within the range only of a professional photographer, like Mike Inman's shot from the Eagle Centre roof.

Another view by the same photographer, repeatable, it appears, only from a hovering balloon, shows the Guildhall and Cathedral towers apparently almost touching but separated by more than that in distance and by 400 years in their building.

There is a tremendous time span covered in walking about Derby. Turn off Sadler Gate and walk down the tunnel that leads into George Yard. Glance right and you see a jumble of building materials that make up the backs of the Iron Gate premises covering hundreds of years.

Turn left and walk down the lane leading to Sadler Gate bridge which nobody's grandparents can remember in place. You may be walking on a track, or so I like to believe, that could have been trodden by citizens of the Danish Royal Borough of Derby.

Most of the photographs in this book were taken by *Evening Telegraph* photographers. A section at the back features pictures taken by readers of the newspaper.

George Yard Lane leads the way down to Sadler Gate.

Picture by Mike Inman.

Shoppers are reduced to the size of ants in this unusual view down Corn Market taken from the tower of Derby Cathedral.

Picture by Martin Elliott.

Good Samaritans stop to help a man who has collapsed in St Peter's Street in the city centre.

Young and old, rich and poor, the city is home to many different people. This image of St Peter's Street captures some of them going about their lives.

A crowd of pigeons in Osnabruck Square in the city centre suddenly takes to the air.

Picture by Mike Inman.

Picture by Sarah Wyatt.

The Market Place pictured at 5am. In just a few hours it will be full of people on their way to work, for now it provides a quiet spot to get some sleep.

Picture by Mike Inman.

Concrete obstacles on the pavement make an interesting feature on Breedon Hill Road.

Picture by Stuart Wilde.

The scene looking down Well Street from North Parade.

Picture by Stuart Wilde.

The view of Bath Street and Rivermead House from North Parade is crowded with buildings and rooftops.

Picture by Stuart Wilde.

The tramway electric switch box on Friar Gate which was used to control the trams run by Derby Corporation Tramways in the city from 1904 to 1932. It is a listed object and has been retained for decorative purposes.

Picture by Stuart Wilde.

Alfreton Road is clearly marked in three different signs, new and old, in this image of an empty shop.

Picture by Stuart Wilde.

The remnants of what used to be a handy resting place for pedestrians near Mansfield Road.

Picture by Mike Inman.

The quintessential English view of a Spitfire and a vintage car in the countryside on the wall of the off licence on the corner of Nightingale Road near the Rolls-Royce works.

The Rolls-Royce works off Addison Road. The site could be mistaken for a military barracks due to its razor-sharp perimeter wire.

A mural on a building off Cotton Lane is a lively addition to an otherwise plain brick wall.

Picture by Mike Inman.

The back of the Vittorio Hair Salon in Littleover which has been almost entirely covered with ivy.

Picture by Stuart Wilde.

What used to be a drinking trough for passing animals on Sitwell Street, Spondon is now a flowerbed to brighten up the area.

Traffic thunders along the raised A52 which runs between the rooftops of Spondon houses in this view from the top of Willowcroft Road.

Picture by Stuart Wilde.

The Markeaton Brook walkway sign points the way to the city centre but has the appearance of a rural setting.

A plain concrete wall has been transformed into an idyllic scene along Markeaton Brook walkway.

The cobbles of Argyle Street glisten in the rain in this view looking towards Burton Road.

Picture by Mike Inman.

The lights in the Eagle Centre seem almost space-age when viewed in black and white as shoppers hurry by.

Picture by Mike Inman.

A man sits back in Osnabruck Square as hundreds of pairs of feet thunder past him daily.

Picture by Mike Inman.

The Guildhall building is protected by the shell-shaped iron castings as seen in this view with the war memorial and Assembly Rooms in the distance.

Picture by Sarah Wyatt.

Busker Lester Norton is silhouetted in the entrance to the Guildhall as the light catches the cobbles.

Picture by Marc Dewhurst.

The rooftops over the stalls in the Guildhall Market.

Light filters through the curved roof over the Guildhall Market. It was made in the county in a similar style to London's St Pancras station roof which was also made in Derbyshire.

Picture by Marc Dewhurst.

Picture by Mike Inman.

The magnificent ceiling of the Guildhall Theatre. It is the original late Regency plaster ceiling of the theatre, built in 1841.

Picture by Mike Inman.

Guildhall Theatre manager Andy Falconer pictured high up inside the building's clock tower.

This ornamental urn on the roof of the Guildhall is usually hidden from view. It is pictured here with Andy Falconer.

The clocks of the Guildhall and the Cathedral in harmony in this shot showing the intricate detail on two of the city's best known buildings.

Picture by Rebecca Russell.

A bird's-eye view of some of the city's major landmarks with the old *Derby Evening Telegraph* building on the right.

Picture by Mike Inman.

Derby's landmark buildings are captured in this unusual view taken from the roof of the Eagle Centre. Pictured from front to back are the Co-op building, the old *Evening Telegraph* building and the Guildhall.

The Co-op cow appears to be walking across the city's rooftops with the old *Evening Telegraph* building on the right.

The sheer size of the Co-op cow can be seen in this image as it dominates the skyline and towers over this rooftop repair man.

A threatening sky over the city with St Mary's church on the left. This image of a thunder storm was captured at 2.30am one Friday night in July.

Picture by Jon Hindmarch.

Cars crowd both sides of Otter Street as the Cathedral (left) and St Mary's church tower over the rooftops.

Picture by Rebecca Russell

Picture by Stuart Wilde.

The old building of the Derby and Derbyshire Banking Company. It was built in 1838 by Robert Wallace of London.

Picture by Mike Inman.

St Luke's church looms over the rooftops of the city in this view from Burton Road,

The ornate chimneys and tower of the College Business Centre on Uttoxeter Road. The building was built in 1851 to the designs of Henry Isaac Stevens of Derby (1807-1873) as the Diocesan (teacher) Training College. The building was added to from 1899 to 1913 and was later part of the Bishop Lonsdale College of Education, later Derby Lonsdale College.

Picture by Mike Inman.

Picture by Stuart Wilde.

The modern white building of the University of Derby is a giant on the horizon in this view down Langley Street towards Peel Street.

Picture by Stuart Wilde.

Mackworth water tower can just be seen through the trees in this view from Prince Charles Avenue.

The huge figure of a knight looms over the entrance to Sims Metal UK on Mansfield Road.

Picture by Rebecca Russell.

Huge powerful machinery is used to deal with 74,000 tonnes of scrap metal every year at Sims Metal UK.

Picture by Jon Hindmarch.

Twins Malcolm (left) and Melvyn Johnson (56) have been crushing cars at Albert Looms scrap yard, Megaloughton Lane, Spondon, since 1960. They were born in Clay Cross and have lived in Chaddesden for most of their lives.

Picture by Johanna De Winter.

Recreating the lives of 10th century Vikings has kept Graham Turner (left) and Nigel Simms busy since 1987. They are pictured here during one of their many school visits.

Picture by Martin Elliott.

The ladies who make the tea and cakes for the Women's Institute. Dorothy Hartley is pictured at the Sherwin Street headquarters.

Green-fingered Jack Litchfield from Allestree is dwarfed by the flowering yucca plant in his garden.

Picture by Johanna De Winter.

Picture by Mike Inman.

People in Allenton are used to seeing the 1958 Rolls Dennis fire engine of Dennis Meynell. He parks it in his front garden and has owned it since 1985.

Picture by Johanna De Winter.

Douglas Bell, who was volunteer curator at the Police Museum on St Mary's Gate for seven years. He looked after one of the largest collections of medals in the country. Sadly, Mr Bell died on July 24, 1999 after a battle with cancer.

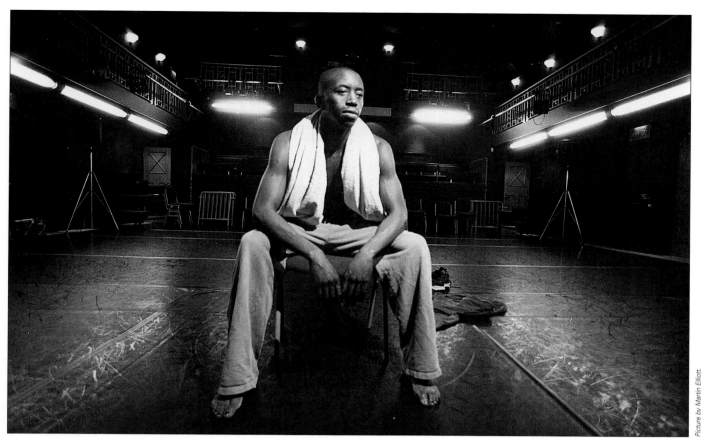

Picture by Martin Elliott.

Dance development worker Leonard Jackson (33) who teaches at Derby Dance Centre on Chapel Street. He has been dancing since his teenage years and trained at the Northern School of Contemporary Dance in Leeds.

Picture by Mike Inman.

Margot Wardle (74) in the garden of her Spondon home which she has transformed into a fairytale cottage. Born in Germany, she moved to the city in 1979.

Three-year-old cart horse Sonny gets a work-out along Meadow Road with his owner farmer John Pegg.

Picture by Martin Elliott.

A portrait of local character Bob Garnett at his home on Langley Street. He is pictured with his much-loved dog Daisy May.

Picture by Mike Inman.

Picture by Martin Elliott.

From song thrushes to Canada geese, 75-year-old Joan Grant knows all there is to know. Joan, a retired air hostess from Grimshaw Avenue, Alvaston, is a dedicated bird lover and has written two books on the subject.

Picture by Stuart Wilde.

Derby County footballer Darryl Powell who has a love of homing pigeons. He has been fascinated by the birds since he was a child growing up in Lambeth. The star is pictured here in the Sinfin Avenue pigeon loft of Anslow Farrar.

Picture by Martin Elliott.

Tai Chi teacher Jeanne Brown (left) practices the ancient Chinese exercise for health and relaxation which, she says, co-ordinates mind, body and spirit. She started learning the art in 1988 and teaches five sessions a week in the city. She is pictured here with pupils Chris Jolly, Ann Horsley, David Green and Carol Greasley.

Picture by Mike Inman.

Allestree golf course provides the frosty setting for these winter golfers.

Picture by Jon Hindmarch.

It is hard to believe that this rural-looking scene on the second fairway of Allestree golf course is no more than five miles from the busy city centre.

Picture by Shelley Buss.

The twice-weekly tea dances at the Assembly Rooms are as popular now as they ever were. Many dancers have been regulars since 1977 when the present Assembly Rooms was opened.

This image of a Flamenco dancing class at Derby Dance Centre on Chapel Street proves that the city is more cosmopolitan than it first appears.

Ladies getting into shape at an aerobics class at St Benedict RC School on Duffield Road.

The Peacock Inn darts team gets in some practice, as it does every Tuesday night at the Nottingham Road pub.

Alex Fernhough (17) and 14-year-old Scott Esplen practice their in-line skating at the skateboarding centre at the Derby Storm training centre on Colombo Street.

Training night at Mickleover Sports Club on Station Road.

A scene which you would expect to find in any country village. This cricket pitch and pavilion however are a stone's throw from the city centre at Parker's Piece.

A hot-air balloon rises high above the Allestree rooftops in this image captured on April 29, 1999.

Picture by Martin Elliott.

Lifeguard Gordon Fearn keeps a watchful eye on swimmers at Queen's Leisure Centre on Cathedral Road.

Not a sight you would expect three miles from a city centre, but the weir at Darley Abbey provides an ideal location for canoeists.

Fred and Hilda Boddy from Castle Gresley ease their barge, *Kotare*, through Stenson Lock. They are both retired and have been travelling on the Trent and Mersey Canal since 1959.

An early morning rower on the River Derwent cuts through the still, mirror-like water leaving a trail of ripples.

The Great Northern Railway bridge built by Andrew Handyside and Co. of Duke Street, Derby, in 1877. It spans the Derwent from Strutt's Park to City Road, Chester Green. As the line closed in 1967, it is now a footbridge and Grade II listed.

Picture by Stuart Wilde.

The cars travelling over the relatively modern St Alkmund's Way contrast with the historic St Mary's Bridge which can be seen behind.

Picture by Stuart Wilde.

Exeter Bridge appears to be almost skimming the swollen River Derwent in this view towards the city centre.

Picture by Johanna De Winter.

The zig-zagging structure of the Spider Bridge over the roundabout on Osmaston Road.

Picture by Mike Inman.

The new cobbles under the bridge to Pride Park catch the sunlight. The beginning of Station Approach can be seen on the right of the picture.

Picture by Shelley Buss.

The modern structure of Pride Park Stadium which became the new home for Derby County Football Club in 1997.

Picture by Sarah Melton.

The car park at Pride Park Stadium is the only large enough space the Derby Serenaders could find to practice on a Sunday morning which would be far enough away not to serenade residents trying to have a weekend lie-in.

Picture by Stuart Wilde.

Pride Park Stadium's head groundsman Mark Robinson makes sure everything is in order for the next match.

Picture by Stuart Wilde.

Eager Rams fans take their seats at Pride Park an hour before their team is due to kick off against Liverpool.

Picture by Stuart Wilde.

Fans mingle around the stadium in anticipation of a win for their team before the match with Liverpool.

Picture by Stuart Wilde

The nets which have seen countless goals already in the Rams' short time at Pride Park are taken down after a match.

The Baseball Ground is almost hidden amongst the rows of terraced houses in the Normanton area of the city, as this view down Cambridge Street shows.

Picture by Shelley Buss.

The rows of seats gather dust in an eerie Baseball Ground since Derby County left for Pride Park in 1997.

A weed has pushed its way through the concrete at the Baseball Ground where thousands of dedicated Rams fans watched them play until their move.

The arched sign points the way to Pear Tree station.

Picture by Jon Hindmarch.

Picture by Jon Hindmarch.

A train thunders along the track towards Pear Tree station.

Picture by Mike Inman.

The new bridge to Pride Park provides the vantage point for this view down the tracks to the platforms of the Midland railway station.

Picture by Mark Radford.

Numbers on the track a short distance from the railway station.

Picture by Stuart Wilde.

A view of the city's industrial-looking skyline as seen from the footbridge over the railway parallel with Mansfield Road.

The same iron footbridge casts angular shadows over the curved surface of the bridge.

Picture by Stuart Wilde.

An artist captures the locomotive *Victory* outside the Industrial Museum on canvas.

The area around the railway track near Raynesway and the A52, as shown here, is easy prey for the city's youths.

Picture by Marc Dewhurst.

Imposing spikes aimed at stopping people getting on to the railway track from Raynesway.

Picture by Stuart Wilde.

The back of a row of old cottages on Highfield Lane, Chaddesden, creates a neat pattern of rooftops.

The remains of the disused railway line over Friar Gate bridge. The line between Ilkeston and Burton-on-Trent was opened by the Great Northern Railway in 1878 and was used up until 1967 when freight travel was discontinued.

Picture by Shelley Buss.

The old platform af Friar Gate station can just be made out although crumbling and overgrown.

Picture by Stuart Wilde.

The mark of Handyside's based in Duke Street, inside the Great Northern Railway Company's Friar Gate bridge which is Grade II listed. Handyside's closed in 1931.

The intricate detail on Friar Gate bridge is captured in the sunlight here. It is often ignored by the hundreds of people that pass under it daily.

Picture by Stuart Wilde.

Pedestrians pass by the now rare red telephone box next to Friar Gate bridge unaware of its status as a Grade II listed building.

This disused railway building at the bottom of Uttoxeter New Road was built in 1877 and was a bonded custom warehouse for the Great Northern Railway used to recieve, store and despatch goods through Friar Gate station. Freight services were discontinued in 1967 but the building remained in use until 1971 to house the rolling stock of the British Rail research section.

Pictures by Mike Inman.

Pictures by Mike Inman.

The Reginald Street baths built in 1904 by borough surveyor John Ward in the Arts and Crafts style. The clock is by John Smith's of Derby. The baths were demolished in the 1980s but the façade was kept.

Picture by Sarah Wyatt.

This clock above the shops on Albion Street was made by Richard Blackwell of English Clockmakers. It was commissioned relatively recently by the developers of the buildings. It is symbolic as it shows views of Derby and railwaymen.

Picture by Stuart Wilde.

Classical decorative columns adorn the NatWest bank on Derwent Street.

What used to be the studios of Victorian photographer Richard Keene on the top floor of a building on Iron Gate.

A wartime lookout has survived over the years on the roof of the old Newton Brothers factory on Alfreton Road.

The relief carvings on the Magistrates' Court building on Derwent Street. It was part of the Central Improvement Scheme of 1932 and was built in 1934. The architect was Charles Aslin (1893-1959) who was borough architect from 1929 to 1945. It is not known whom Aslin commissioned to carve the panels, although he probably designed them himself.

Built in 1906, 32 Iron Gate replaced the former house of John 'Equity' Wright, father of Joseph Wright (1734-1797), which was demolished the year before.

A beautiful lamppost near the Industrial Museum.

Picture by Mike Inman.

The Silk Mill gates, which are Grade II listed, were made in 1724 by Robert Bakewell of Derby (1682-1752), England's greatest native-born wrought-iron smith. Between 1934 and 1988, they stood beside the library in the Wardwick.

Picture by Mike Inman.

Iron Gate is reflected in the circular surface of a city centre camera put in place to keep a watchful eye on goings on.

Picture by Mike Inman.

The words 'motor cars' on the Rolls-Royce building on Nightingale Road are a reminder of a past era when cars were made in the city.

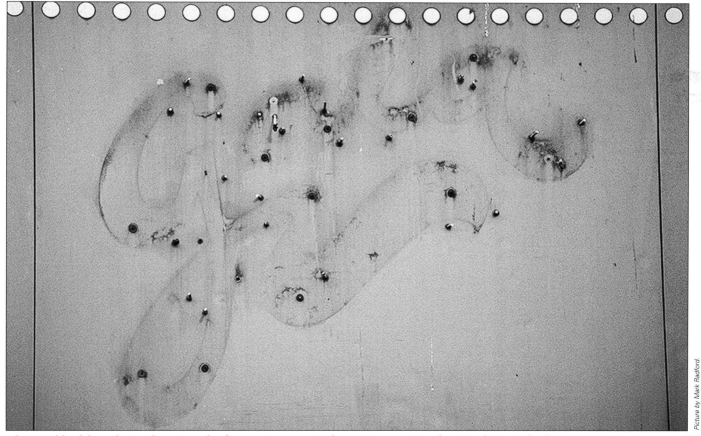

Picture by Mark Radford.

The word 'Gala' can be made out on the former Gaumont Palace cinema on London Road. It was built in 1934 to the designs of A.E. Jay. It was bought by T. Arthur Rank in 1941 and was the Odeon between 1965 and 1983 and became the new Trocadero in 1983. It was then used for bingo until its closure. In 1999 it was the subject of plans to turn it into a nightspot.

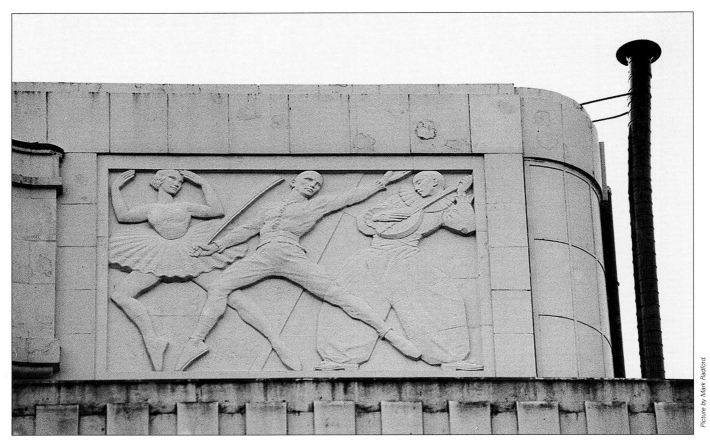

Picture by Mark Radford.

The relief sculpture on the side of the former Gaumont Palace building hints at one of its many uses over the years.

Picture by Mark Radford.

The words 'Thurman and Malin' can just be made out on the wall high above McDonald's on St Peter's Street. The business was founded in the street in 1879 by William Malin and John Thurman, it was described in 1891 as a "drapers, hosiers and undertakers". The firm closed in about 1970. The premises on St Peter's Street now occupied by McDonald's were built in 1896/7 as an early department store.

A detail from the drum tower of a building on the corner of St Peter's Street and St Peter's Churchyard. It shows carved classical figures probably from the 1890s. The building may have belonged to Boots before the shop moved across the road.

Two carved decorative lions keep watch over the old Post Office on Victoria Street.

Signs in the window of the old Gaumont Palace cinema on London Road.

Above and right: The original Boots building in the Arts and Crafts style on the corner of St Peter's Street and East Street. It was built in 1912 by Albert Nelson Bromley of Nottingham and is covered in plaster decoration called pargetting which was an East Anglian craft. It has statues of four famous Derby people set into the sides made by Morley Horder.

FLORENCE · NIGHTINGALE

Picture by Mike Inman.

This image shows the level that the water reached during the flood of 1842. It is on the wall of the Wardwick Inn, The Wardwick.

Picture by Mike Inman.

Light pours in through the glass roof over the Strand Arcade. The arcade was the final element in the Strand development.

These gates tell the story of Cox and Malin, the city's biggest vintners. The business was established in 1763 in the Market Place and in 1876, when Iron Gate was widened, the building, which is now a bar, was built.

The relief decoration on the wall around the River Gardens is an interesting feature which is often overlooked.

Picture by Mike Inman.

This image shows part of the original ceiling which was in the building on the Market Place which was a townhouse for the Duke of Newcastle. The ceiling, made in 1680, was placed in the room in which Charles I had been entertained in 1636. When the present Assembly Rooms was built between 1971 and 1977, part of the ceiling was saved and put in the new building.

Picture by Johanna De Winter.

The intricate plasterwork on the ceiling of what is now La Tosca restaurant on London Road. It was built in 1913 as the Cosy Cinema which closed in 1951 when the building became a shop.

Picture by Stuart Wilde.

The Spondon Co-operative Grocer and Butchery was purpose-built in 1897 by the Derby Co-operative Society. As this image shows, it is now an Indian takeaway.

Picture by Rebecca Russell.

A mixture of old and new appears in this image. An old-fashioned sign points the way to the cattle market above the Five Lamps Tandoori sign.

The unusual tower on Five Lamps Nursing Home at the bottom of Duffield Road stands out above the trees.

Picture by Martin Elliott.

The auction is a tense time for buyers at Derby Cattle Market based at West Meadows.

Picture by Martin Elliott.

It is almost as if you have stepped back in time as you enter the cattle market which has been running at West Meadows since 1965, although there has been a cattle market in the city for centuries.

Picture by Stuart Wilde.

John and Carole Waring pictured outside the butcher's shop which they have run for the last 30 years on the corner of Langley Street and Handford Street.

Picture by Martin Elliott.

Jack Marcer began working as a baker in 1976 with 12 pounds in the till and two pounds of flour. Now he employs most of his family in the business. Pictured with Jack are gran Hazel Trowell, Jack's wife Susan, their son Gary, his wife Marissa and their daughter Chelsea, Jack's daughter Elizabeth Green, her husband Stuart and their daughter Charlotte Ellen. Also pictured are staff Danny Quemby, Steve Baker and Carl Peach. The business now uses one and a half tonnes of flour a week.

The gates to the fish market in Lock-Up Yard. The market moved to its present site from Osnabruck Square in the late 1980s when the gates were put in place.

John Andrews has been getting up at 4am since 1969 in order to set up his stall selling everything from lobsters to cod at the city's fish market in Lock-Up Yard.

Picture by Sarah Melton.

Curry chef at the Shalimar Tandoori restaurant on Midland Road, Ashraf Muhammed prepares for a busy evening by setting out all the ingredients he will need.

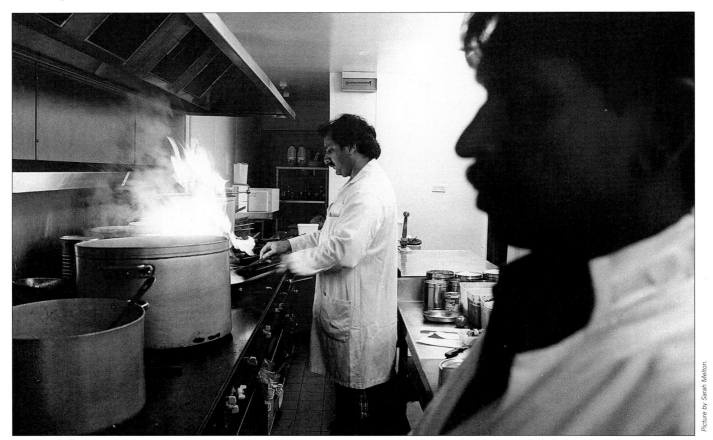

Picture by Sarah Melton.

A glimpse inside the kitchen at the Shalimar Tandoori restaurant. Curry chef Ashraf Muhammed (left) is pictured hard at work with tandoori chef Jamil Hamed.

Mick Barnes serves up breakfast at 6am to the regulars at Uncle Tom's Cabin in Osnabruck Square.

Meofitos Evriviades, the manager of the Britannia coffee bar on East Street. He has been in the coffee shop business in the city since 1967.

Picture by Johanna De Winter.

Sandy Cameron works on the mountain of washing up at Asterdale Primary School, Borrowash.

Picture by Martin Elliott.

Even in the summer holidays, there is no time to rest for Jane Holden, head of the sixth form at Littleover Community School.

Picture by Martin Elliott.

While the pupils are away during the summer break the cleaners get to work to give the building a thorough spruce up at Littleover Community School.

Every morning, six days a week, since 1987, 77-year-old Adam Appleby has cleaned the tables at Riley's 24-hour snooker hall on Mansfield Road.

Gerry Connely inspects the city's sewer shaft as people pass by on the street above him.

Picture by Stuart Wilde.

This is the sight that all rats try to avoid, the council's pest controller Clive Mosley whose job it is to rid the city of vermin.

Picture by Marc Dewhurst.

The window of Headlines wigs and hairpieces shop on Market Place. It opened in 1978 managed by Hazel Malia. She bought the shop in 1981 and has many loyal customers who have been coming in since it opened.

Picture by Sarah Wyatt.

Hazel Malia makes some final adjustments to a wig in her shop.

Picture by Sarah Wyatt.

Derby-born Steven Derrick (45) of S.A. Derrick, Clock and Watch Repairs, has been helping the people of Derby arrive on time since the Sixties. He is pictured in his workshop at his Littleover home.

Taxi controller Brian Milner at the nerve centre of Derby firm 75 Taxis, based on Ascot Drive.

Picture by Steve Baker.

Garage attendant Dave West working the night shift at the Shell petrol station on Ashbourne Road.

Picture by Sarah Melton.

Picture by Sarah Melton.

A Group 4 security officer keeps watch over the Rolls-Royce sites during the night.

Picture by Sarah Wyatt.

Derby-born artist Paul Gregory pictured in his Spondon studio. He has been creating artwork for heavy metal album covers since 1984.

Picture by Sarah Wyatt.

Tattooist Wayne Brockhurst deep in concentration as he works on an intricate design at Tattoo Sensations, Nottingham Road, Chaddesden.

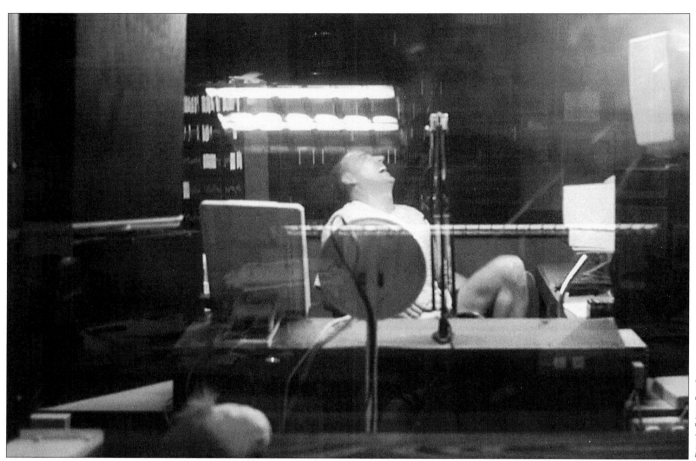

Picture by Rebecca Russell.

People often hear him, but few ever see DJ Andy Miller, pictured here presenting Ram FM's breakfast show.

Picture by Johanna De Winter.

Senior film studies technician David Gold changes the spool of film in the projection room at the Metro cinema on Green Lane.

Picture by Johanna De Winter.

David Gold winds back the spools of film in the projection room at the Metro.

Picture by Jon Hindma

The latest releases are added to the display every week by staff at the UCI cinema on Mansfield Road.

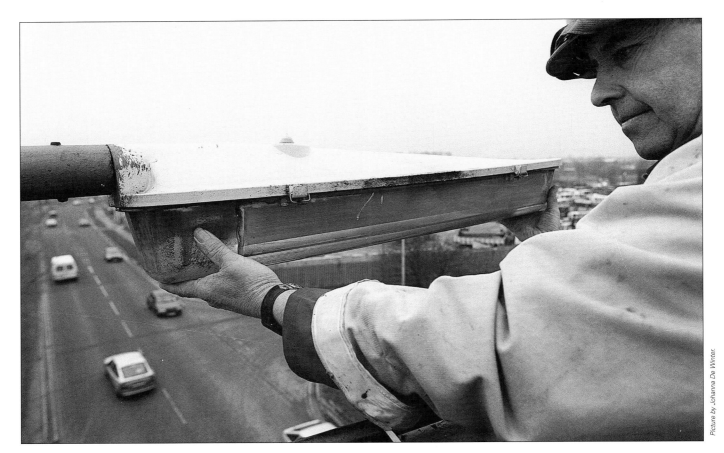

Dave Wright helps to shed some light on the city's streets by maintaining the street lights. He is seen here working in Ascot Drive. Mr Wright has worked for Derby City Council contractor services since the Seventies and is their longest-serving employee.

Derby City Council worker Darrell Bolton helps to take care of the city's toilets. Every hour, six days a week, he cleans the facilities at the Eagle Centre and The Spot.

Picture by Stuart Wilde.

The new recruits of Derbyshire Fire and Rescue Service training at Kingsway fire station.

Picture by Sarah Melton.

Chambermaid Anna Carson makes sure everything is spick-and-span in room 119 at the Midland Hotel, Midland Road.

Picture by Stuart Wilde.

Quick fingers are needed as the local election votes are counted at St Mary's School on Darley Lane.

Picture by Martin Elliott.

Celebrations fill the air at this Hindu wedding festival at the Assembly Rooms.

Julia Inger in the doorway of the Chester Green newsagents which her family has owned since the Fifties.

Picture by Jon Hindmarch.

George Virk, shopkeeper at the Londis shop, Browning Circle, Sinfin.

Picture by Sarah Melton.

Trainee pharmacist Ben Eaton carefully counts pills into a bottle at the Dean and Smedley chemist on Prince Charles Avenue, Mackworth.

Signs of the times at Elvaston Castle as preparations get under way for the 120th County Show.

Car park attendant Pete Carter in his office off Full Street.

The chains to stop over height vehicles going under the bridge on Nottingham Road are made easier to see with a lick of bright paint.

Volunteer Albert Hibbert measures clothes which have been donated to the Help the Aged charity shop on Babington Lane.

Volunteers Michelle Slack (left) and Sally Winter hard at work helping out in the kitchen of the Padley Day Centre on Beckett Street. The centre aims to help the homeless and disadvantaged in Derby to improve their self esteem and help them integrate with the community.

Colin Graham pictured at the Padley Day Centre, where he attends for help and support.

Picture by Mark Radford.

Lydia's fabric stall on the Eagle Centre Market which is run by Lydia Ball. She is pictured with one of her many rolls of fabric.

Picture by Sarah Melton.

The Eagle Centre Market closing down after a hard day's work. Fiona Hogan is pictured clearing up on Frank Woodhouse's fruit and veg stall.

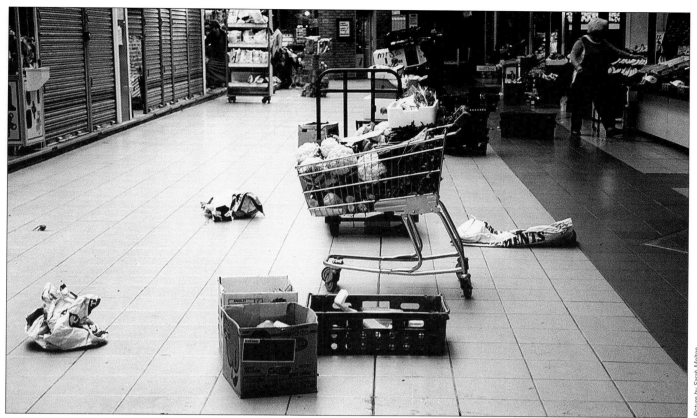

Picture by Sarah Melton.

Market traders close down their stalls after a day's work.

Picture by Rebecca Russell.

A huge digger is used delicately amongst the headstones to dig graves in Nottingham Road cemetery.

An angel guards the headstone of Unetti Hamer in Nottingham Road cemetery. She was known as the Queen of the gypsies. The cemetery has traditionally become a place where many Romany gypsies have been buried over the years.

The grave of Derby County and England footballing legend Steve Bloomer nestles among others in Nottingham Road cemetery.

Another suspected gypsy grave in Nottingham Road cemetery. Joseph Smith, among others, is buried here. The sheer grandeur of the grave indicates that it is a gypsy burial site.

Picture by Johanna De Winter.

The Robert Pegg monument, recently given Grade II listed status, stands tall in the Uttoxeter New Road cemetery. Robert Pegg was the Mayor of Derby from 1855-1856 and the founder of Pegg's colour works in the Morledge. He built Osmaston Road Baptist Church, since replaced, and the elaborate Melbourne House next to it.

Picture by Mike Inman.

Picture by Mike Inman.

The tombstone of Derby artist Joseph Wright (1734-1797) at the side of the Cathedral. The artist was originally buried at St Alkmund's Church which was demolished to make way for the ring road. The remains in the Wright family grave were moved to Nottingham Road cemetery and the tombstone was placed in Cathedral grounds in 1997.

Picture by Sarah Wyatt.

The beautifully shaped windows in the tower of Derby Cathedral provide a bird's-eye view of the city centre.

Picture by Sarah Wyatt.

St Katherine's Chapel in Derby Cathedral is a peaceful place for quiet prayer and meditation. It was named after St Katherine of Alexandria who was tortured on a wheel and hence gave her name to the Katherine Wheel. The present building was consecrated as a cathedral in 1927 but the foundations date back to the 10th century when it was a Saxon Christian site.

Picture by Shelley Buss.

Father Jim Burke, assistant priest of St Mary's Church, Darley Lane, and Holy Family Church, Allestree, in the Blessed Sacrament Chapel which was formerly a stage for performances at the Holy Family Church building.

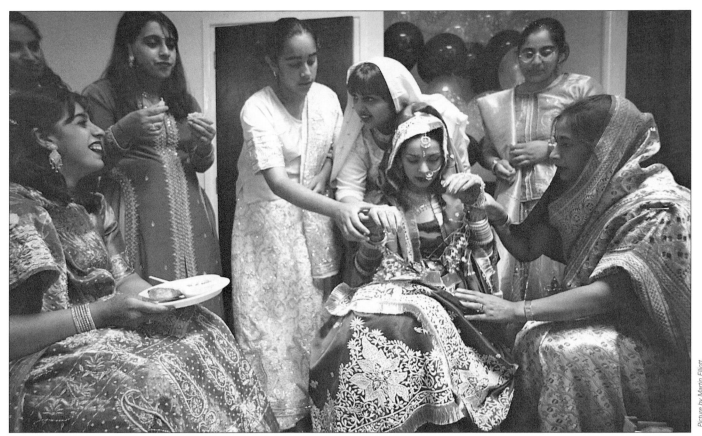

The bride at a Sikh wedding having her hands painted with henna at her henna party before the ceremony at the Sikh Temple on Normanton Road.

Picture by Martin Elliott.

The bride and bridegroom sit at the altar during the Sikh ceremony at the temple.

Picture by Martin Elliott.

Sisters Francis and Monica have a quiet moment of prayer in the Sisters of Mercy private chapel on Bridge Gate.

Picture by Steve Baker.

Picture by Steve Baker.

The Bishop of Derby, the Right Reverend Jonathan Bailey, at a service in St Mary's Church, Darley Lane.

Picture by Martin Elliott.

The open air mass led by the Right Reverend Timothy Wright reflected in the windows of St Benedict RC School on Duffield Road.

The Cathedral is duplicated in this image reflected in a shop window on Queen Street.

Picture by Mike Inman.

St Mary's Church, built in 1839, reflected in the tinted windows of offices which look out on to King Street.

All angles of Sadler Gate are reflected in the mirrors of this shop window.

A bird's-eye view of Sadler Gate from the attic of the Old Bell Inn.

The Old Bell Inn on Sadler Gate hides a 17th-century dog kennels where the guard dogs for the coaches were housed. This was also home for the stable boys.

Old fashioned signs outside shops and pubs along an alleyway off Sadler Gate in the city centre.

Picture by Marc Dewhurst.

Picture by Johanna De Winter.

The worn cobbles of George Yard off Sadler Gate have been walked over by generations of Derbeians.

Picture by Mike Inman.

Council worker Nick Manning cleans off graffiti from the city's walls.

The graffiti on a wall in the River Gardens near the Council House speaks for itself.

Graffiti sprayed under East Gate bridge as a bus thunders past.

Picture by Jon Hindmarch.

Bus driver Dave Ward changes places with Lynn Walker at the Trent buses driver change-over point at the end of Meadow Road.

Picture by Stuart Wilde.

To the users of the bus station, the two old clocks are an invaluable part of the furniture, one of which is shown here.

After countless journeys around the city's streets, the Arriva buses are cleaned off at the depot on Ascot Drive.

Picture by Martin Elliott.

Picture by Martin Elliott.

Making Arriva buses spotless is Ellen Castledine's job.

Picture by Stuart Wilde.

A bus makes a winding journey through the Breadsall estate.

Picture by Johanna De Winter.

An image of surburban Derby, the almost identical houses on Broughton Avenue, Littleover.

Picture by Stuart Wilde.

Two cottages which have been surrounded by modern industrial buildings over the years.

Picture by Stuart Wilde.

A disused building nestles amongst the trees in a corner of Darley Park just inside the South Drive entrance.

Picture by Stuart Wilde.

The backs of the houses on Otter Street facing Darley Park and the river.

Picture by Stuart Wilde.

The celebrated 18th-century Venetian fountain which was brought back by one of the Mundy family from the Grand Tour and placed in the grounds of Markeaton Hall. It was sold by the council when the hall was demolished and subsequently acquired by Dr Hamilton, then of Matlock Bath. He offered it back to the council three times and the third time it was accepted on condition it was placed in Darley Park where Dr Hamilton could see it from his nearby house.

Picture by Stuart Wilde.

A detail on the fountain.

Picture by Mike Inman.

A countryside scene in the heart of a city, Darley Park seen through the railings of the terrace café.

Picture by Stuart Wilde.

An old lodge house at the entrance to the stables and courtyard at Elvaston Castle. Its style and unusual design suggest that it was built as part of William Barron's redesign of the gardens between 1820 and 1850. It would have been lived in by an estate worker and his family. Rumour has it that a family with 16 children once lived there.

Picture by Martin Elliott.

Elvaston Castle Museum demonstrator Ann Torr takes a step back in time to the turn of the last century. She is pictured in the wash house at the museum where she shows visitors how the mangle was used when the family laundry was done there.

Picture by Martin Elliott.

Stockman at Elvaston Castle Farm, John Simnett, takes a well-earned break between jobs as Blossom the pig sunbathes in her pen.

Picture by Mike Inman.

One of two ornamental turtles in Allestree Park. The turtles started life in the River Gardens. They were then moved to Markeaton Park in about 1972 where they became buried under bark and woodchippings in the woodyard. They remained hidden for a few years before being uncovered and placed in the pond in Allestree Park.

Picture by Mike Inman.

Not unusual on the plains of Africa, but the sight of three rhinos strolling through Markeaton Park is slightly out of the ordinary. They are wood carvings made from a tree which was chopped down in the park.

Picture by Martin Elliott.

All the seasons blend into one for the resident cats at Markeaton Glasshouses. They live in a temperature-controlled environment all year round.

Picture by Rebecca Russell.

A swan and her cygnets sit peacefully in the middle of Markeaton Brook.

The owl on the base of the statue of Florence Nightingale on London Road, near Derbyshire Royal Infirmary. There is a story that she used to carry an owl in her pocket whilst on her rounds, however this is unlikely. The owl is a symbol of vigilance and this may have related to her work, a lot of which was at night. The Grade II listed statue was erected in 1924 and was carved by Countess Gleichen (1862-1922) in about 1912. Florence Nightingale (1820-1910) was born at Lea Hurst and later advised on the rebuilding of the former General Infirmary in the 1860s.

Picture by Mark Radford.

The statue of Michael Thomas Bass (1799-1884) behind Derby Museum and Art Gallery. Bass was MP for Derby in 1848-1883 and a great benefactor to the city. Bass was the third generation Burton brewer of his family and expanded the firm greatly, making it a household name. The statue was unveiled in the Market Place in 1884 but was moved in 1924.

Picture by Rebecca Russell.

The war memorial on Midland Road which is Grade II listed. It was made in 1921 by Edwin Lutyens to remember the Midland Railway workers who lost their lives in the First World War. It has an unusual whiteness as it is made from Portland stone.

Picture by Rebecca Russell.

A war memorial on the side of St Michael's Church bearing the dates 1914 and 1918, the dates of the First World War.

A life-like statue on the side of St Mary's Church on Darley Lane.

Picture by Rebecca Russell.

PLAN OF
THE FREE LIBRARY
DERBY

A detail of the Bass statue.

Bonnie Prince Charlie is immortalised in this statue on Full Street. HRH Prince Charles Edward Stuart (1720-1788) was the grandson of the deposed James II and made a near successful attempt to regain the throne for the Stuarts in 1745. He came to Derby for two days in December 1745 and lodged at Exeter House, now demolished, near the statue.

The clock and weather vane on the old stable block at the council's Stores Road depot. The stables were originally built to house the horses and carts used for refuse collection in the city. Rubbish lorries, gritters and recycling lorries are still operating from the original site.

Picture by Shelley Buss.

Labourer Dominic Doherty sweeps up in the old stable block.

Picture by Shelley Buss.

Picture by Stuart Wilde.

Plastic bottles destined for recycling are sifted out of the rubbish at the council's Stores Road depot. Last year, Derby City Council handled 149.5 tonnes of different types of plastics which were recycled into anything from buckets to duvet fillings and protective tubes for trees.

Picture by Stuart Wilde.

Bottles wait to be recycled at the depot.

Richard Langley from the Museum and Art Gallery inspects an old photographic enlarger lens at the storeroom which is packed with artefacts.

The Museum and Art Gallery storeroom which houses thousands of artefacts including the entire contents of a chemist's shop.

Picture by Steve Baker.

Huge amounts of knowledge gathers dust in the storeroom which houses many books.

Picture by Steve Baker.

Richard Langley in one of the aisles of the storeroom.

The storeroom where lost, confiscated and recovered property is housed at Cotton Lane police station.

Picture by Mike Inman.

The collection of air rifles stored at Cotton Lane police station which have been confiscated by officers.

Picture by Mike Inman.

Picture by Martin Elliott.

PCs Dean Frost and Simon Bulmer are trained firearms officers who drive Derby's Armed Response Vehicle which is called out to any incident where firearms have been reported.

Picture by Martin Elliott

A man is charged while his legal representative looks on in the custody suite at Full Street police station.

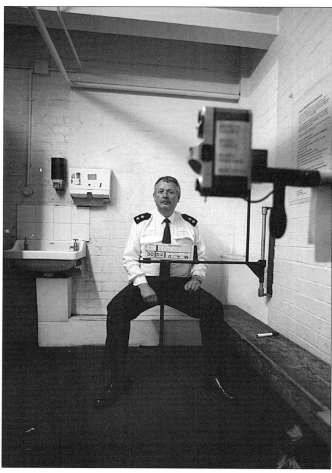

Abovel left: Sergeant Mick Goacher pictured at his desk in the control room of Full Street police station.

Abovel right: Inspector Bob Smith pictured in Full Street police station where mug shots of prisoners are taken.

Tom Houlston has been responsible for cleaning out the cells at Full Street police station since 1986.

Communications officer Phil Blood on the roof of Full Street police station.

The brand new Toyota cars at the Burnaston plant look like toy cars in this view from the air.

Picture by Steve Baker.

A Trent 895 engine used on British Airways planes and made at Rolls-Royce in Derby.

Picture by Mike Inman.

The windows of an old mill form an abstract pattern as seen in this view from Willow Row.

The view from the tower on the Masonic Lodge in Littleover. It was built in 1829 to allow the owner at the time to spy on the workers at his Litchurch foundry to check that they were not slacking off.

Picture by Johanna De Winter.

The tower on the Masonic Lodge building.

Below: The Liversage Trust almshouses on London Road. The Liversage Trust was the wealthiest charity in Derby, founded by Robert Liversage in the 16th century.

Picture by Johanna De Winter.

Picture by Mike Inman.

One of the oldest surviving chapels in Derby is on Brook Street. It was built in 1802 as the General Baptist Chapel and rebuilt in its present form in 1856 as a Wesley chapel. It is a listed building and the gates are hand-made wrought iron. The 'wiggly' bars are typical of Robert Bakewell although they are not thought to be by him.

Picture by Johanna De Winter.

Picture by Mark Radford.

The shadow of an old-fashioned street light is cast on to a wall behind the museum.

The toll bridge at Darley Abbey.

A view of Derbyshire County Cricket Club's ground off the Pentagon Island.

A stone carving at the County Ground bearing the date 1911.

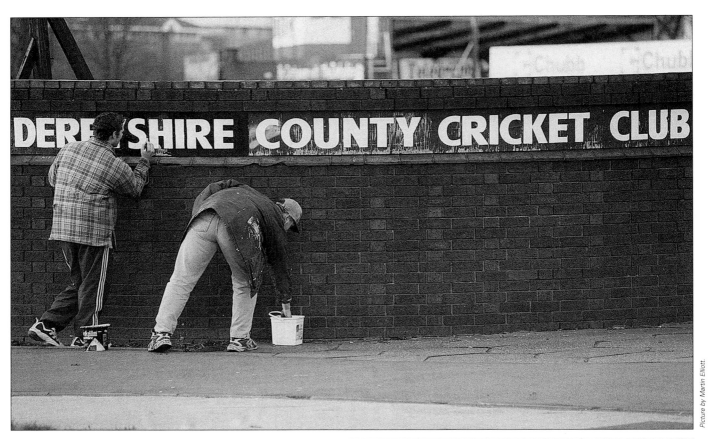

The signs at the County Ground are given a lick of paint in preparation for the new season in April.

The floor is given a polish at the Derby Storm basketball arena.

Picture by Martin Elliott.

George Cannon, a part-time cleaner at the Derby Storm basketball arena, clears up after a game.

Picture by Steve Baker.

The Friar Gate Launderette which is open seven days a week from 8.30am until 9pm. It has been owned by the King family since 1972. It has been a launderette since 1952 and is thought to have been the first in Derby.

Window cleaner Lee Evans at the top of Derbyshire Royal Infirmary above Accident and Emergency on a hydraulic platform.

One of the always busy corridors at the DRI.

Two theatre nurses at the DRI pose for the camera from a third-storey window in this light-hearted moment.

Readers' Pictures

An image of an artist on the streets of the city.

A picture entitled *Spider Bridge Boy.*

Picture by Matt Partridge from Derby.

Markeaton Brook with an iron bridge
over it.

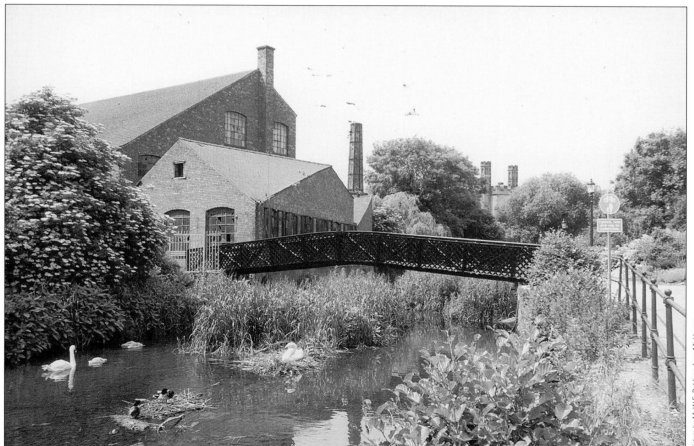

Picture by Mr W.F. Boldison from Mickleover.

Picture by David Siddons from Fritchley.

Three of the city's characters.

Picture by Matt Partridge from Derby.

The Venue on Wilson Street.

Picture by Brenda Ray from Mickleover.

The hats in a shop window with an interesting reflection.

A view over the city from Babington Lane.

Picture by David Siddons from Fritchley.

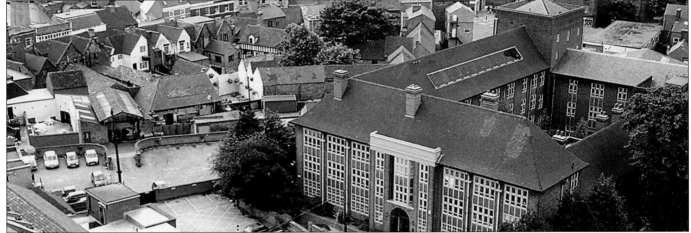

Picture by Kaffe Mannion from Derby.

The city crowded with buildings in this view.

Old and new buildings within a stone's throw of each other in Green Lane.

Picture by Christian Philippi.

Picture by Paul Mileman from Derby.

A picture that appears to go on for eternity.

Picture by Brenda Ray from Mickleover.

The steps to Markeaton Hall captured on film.

The little girl in this picture was captured on film by Matt Partridge.

Picture by Paul Milleman from Derby.

An image from a night out in the city.

Picture by Brenda Ray from Mickleover.

Old iron columns still standing by the River Derwent.

A telephone engineer works on the streets of Derby in the evening sunshine.

David Owen from Chester Green captured this interesting image looking down the river.

Picture by David Owen.

Removal men take a
well-earned tea break in
this photograph.

Picture by Karen Harnaway from Mickleover.